D1621679

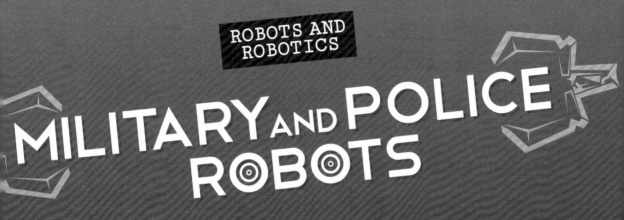

ROBOTS AND ROBOTICS

MILITARY AND POLICE ROBOTS

DANIEL R. FAUST

PowerKiDS
press.

New York

Published in 2017 by The Rosen Publishing Group, Inc.
29 East 21st Street, New York, NY 10010

First Edition

Editor: Caitie McAneney
Book Design: Reann Nye

Photo Credits: Cover Ed Darack/Science Faction/Getty Images; p. 4 Laslo Ludrovan/Shutterstock.com; p. 5 daseaford/Shutterstock.com; p. 6 Stacy Barnett/Shutterstock.com; p. 7 ProstoSvet/Shutterstock.com; p. 8 fluke samed/Shutterstock.com; p. 9 JOHANNES EISELE/AFP/Getty Images; p. 10 https:// en.wikipedia.org/wiki/File:Sdkfz302elektr.jpg; p. 11 Interim Archives/Archive Photos/Getty Images; p. 12 https://commons.wikimedia.org/wiki/File:Arati_Prabhakar_DARPA_Aug_2012.jpg; p. 13 https:// commons.wikimedia.org/wiki/File:Tadiran-Mastiff-III-hatzerim-1.jpg; p. 16 MASSOUD HOSSAINI/AFP/ Getty Images; p. 17 https://commons.wikimedia.org/wiki/File:Raven_UAV.jpg; p. 19 (Raven) https:// commons.wikimedia.org/wiki/File:RQ-11_Raven_1.jpg; p. 19 (Shadow) https://commons.wikimedia. org/wiki/File:Shadow_200_UAV_(2).jpg; p. 19 (Global Hawk) https://commons.wikimedia.org/wiki/ File:Global_Hawk_1.jpg; p. 20 https://commons.wikimedia.org/wiki/File:IRobot_PackBot_510_E.T..JPG; p. 21 https://commons.wikimedia.org/wiki/File:US_Navy_120125-N-MT220-046_A_Sailor_shows_an_ elementary_school_student_class_how_to_maneuver_a_Talon_robot.jpg; p. 23 https://commons.wikimedia. org/wiki/File:SWORDS_robot.jpg; p. 25 https://commons.wikimedia.org/wiki/File:USMC-091204-M-3876F-003.jpg; p. 26 Valentin Valkov/Shutterstock.com; p. 27 THOMAS SAMSON/AFP/Getty Images; p. 28 https://commons.wikimedia.org/wiki/File:Black_Hornet_Nano_Helicopter_UAV.jpg; p. 29 courtesy of the U.S. Navy; p. 30 https://commons.wikimedia.org/wiki/File:US_Army_ powered_armor.jpg.

Library of Congress Cataloging-in-Publication Data

Names: Faust, Daniel R., author.
Title: Military and police robots / Daniel R. Faust.
Description: New York : PowerKids Press, [2016] | Series: Robots and robotics
  | Includes index.
Identifiers: LCCN 2016011878 | ISBN 9781499421781 (pbk.) | ISBN 9781499421804 (library bound)
| ISBN 9781499421798 (6 pack)
Subjects: LCSH: Military robots–Juvenile literature. | Robots–Juvenile
  literature.
Classification: LCC UG450 .F38 2016 | DDC 355.8–dc23
LC record available at http://lccn.loc.gov/2016011878

Manufactured in the United States of America

CPSIA Compliance Information: Batch #BS16PK: For Further Information contact Rosen Publishing, New York, New York at 1-800-237-9932

CONTENTS

EXCITING NEW TECHNOLOGY

When you imagine police and military robots, you probably think of a battlefield full of humanlike robots fighting each other. This kind of futuristic robot army has been featured in Hollywood movies and TV shows. The robots of today may be more advanced than those that came before them, but we're still many years away from armies of humanlike robot soldiers.

Engineers are developing exciting robotic technology for the police and military. Today, **drones** fly over enemy territory to gather important information or attack out-of-the-way targets. Bomb disposal robots disarm or get rid of explosives from a safe distance. There are even remote-controlled robots that look like small tanks. Each robot greatly helps the police and military in their missions.

They may not look like Hollywood's idea of robot soldiers, but today's military robots fight alongside our troops in some of the most dangerous, or unsafe, places in the world.

ROBOT MEDICS

Robots are used to fill many roles in today's military. Now, the U.S. Army is interested in developing new robots for medical uses. Wounded soldiers need to be removed from the battlefield and given medical attention as soon as possible. Unmanned ambulances could get these soldiers to safety without risking the lives of human medics. Robot medics could also deliver medical supplies to soldiers working in enemy territory. The faster a soldier receives medical attention and supplies, the better chance they have of surviving an injury or illness.

Military and police robots come in many shapes and sizes. Some are built for the ground, while others are aerial, or operating in the air. Whatever these robots might look like, most share the same basic components, or parts. The basic parts of a robot are effectors, actuators, sensors, and the control system, or controller.

This robot arm is used to move bombs and **mines**. The actuators at each joint move the arm into position, while another actuator moves the effector to grasp an object, such as a bomb.

QUADCOPTER

The effectors and actuators are a robot's moving parts. Effectors are the parts of a robot that interact directly with its surroundings. They allow a robot to perform specific tasks, such as lifting and moving objects. Gripper claws, hammers, shovels, and screwdrivers are examples of effectors. Actuators are the motors that power the effectors. They also power the parts that make a robot move, such as wheels and treads. Quadcopter drones have four propellers, and an actuator powers each one.

Sensors gather information about a robot's surroundings. The simplest robots have sensors that prevent them from hitting obstacles, such as walls, furniture, or people. Other robots have cameras and microphones that act just like your eyes and ears. Some robots can see and hear better than you can. Some military and police robots are equipped with special sensors that allow them to detect temperature, air pressure, **radiation** levels, and changes to Earth's gravity or magnetic field.

Many police and military robots, such as this drone, have video cameras they use as sensors, providing real-time video of the robot's surroundings.

The final basic component of any robot is the controller. The controller processes information about the robot's surroundings using information gathered through the sensors. Then it moves the robot according to a series of preprogrammed actions. Other robots are controlled remotely, or from a distance, by an operator.

MILITARY ROBOT HISTORY

Robot soldiers are still a thing of the future, but militaries around the world have been using robots for quite some time. During World War II, the German army used the remote-controlled Goliath vehicle. The Goliath was steered remotely by a **joystick** control box. It could carry more than 130 pounds (59 kg) of explosives. The Goliath was used against tanks, bridges, buildings, and enemy soldiers.

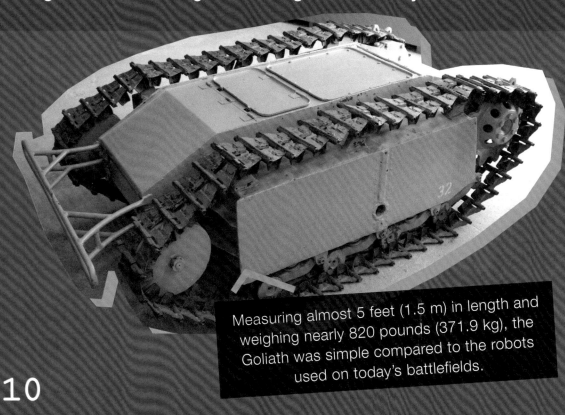

Measuring almost 5 feet (1.5 m) in length and weighing nearly 820 pounds (371.9 kg), the Goliath was simple compared to the robots used on today's battlefields.

The Germans weren't the only **combatants** to use robots during World War II. The Soviet Union created remote-controlled unmanned tanks called teletanks. Teletanks had flamethrowers and machine guns, and some carried special timed bombs. The Goliath vehicles and teletanks were able to get closer to the enemy with less risk to the people who controlled them.

The military robots you're probably most familiar with are drones, which are officially called unmanned aerial vehicles, or UAVs. Drones have become a popular military tool in recent years, but militaries have been using other aerial tools for much longer.

Countries have long used balloons and kites to take aerial photographs. Balloons were also used to drop bombs on enemies, and they were even used for

DARPA

The Defense Advanced Research Projects Agency, or DARPA, is an agency within the United States Department of Defense. DARPA was founded in 1958 as a reaction to the Soviet Union's *Sputnik*, which was the first man-made satellite launched into space. DARPA is responsible for the development of new and emerging technologies. Although developed for the military, many of DARPA's scientific breakthroughs in the areas of medicine, robotics, and computer science have been made available to the public.

DR. ARATI PRABHAKAR
THE HEAD OF DARPA

One of the first modern battlefield drones was the Mastiff, which was created by Tadiran Electronic Industries in 1975 for the Israeli military.

reconnaissance in the American Civil War. The Vietnam War saw advancements to drone warfare. Drones made it possible to fly over enemy territory and gather **intelligence** without risking the lives of human pilots.

During World War I, the United States developed an unmanned aerial torpedo called the Kettering Bug. It was essentially a flying bomb that could hit a target miles away.

ROBOTS ON THE BATTLEFIELD

Some robots on today's battlefields may look similar to the German Goliath or the Soviet teletank. However, advances in technology allow modern military robots to do so much more. Like human soldiers, military robots fill many different roles. There are large robots used to carry equipment, robots designed to handle dangerous materials, and small robots that are used for **surveillance** and reconnaissance.

Military robots can operate on land or in the air. UAVs fly over battlefields, taking aerial photographs or real-time video. Some UAVs can even be used for combat missions. Unmanned ground vehicles, or UGVs, are a lot like their flying cousins. Both operate without a human controller on board. UAVs and UGVs are controlled remotely using either a handheld controller or a command **console**.

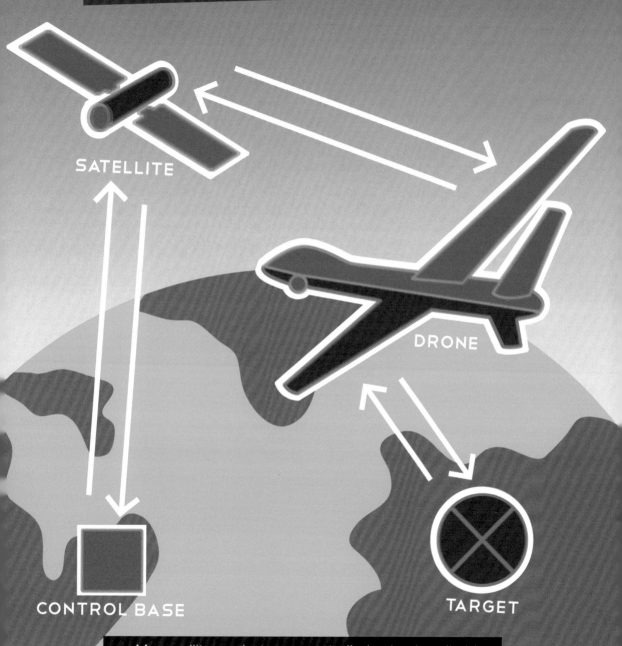

HOW DO MILITARY DRONES WORK?

SATELLITE

DRONE

CONTROL BASE

TARGET

Many military robots are controlled using handheld devices similar to what you might use to control a toy car or airplane. More complex robots require controls that resemble laptops or full-size computers.

EYES IN THE SKY

The military often uses drones for reconnaissance and surveillance. Military drones can be equipped with still cameras and video cameras. They also can have special sensors with which to see in the dark and poor weather conditions. The information provided by drones has the potential to save the lives of human soldiers, as well as innocent **civilians**.

PREDATOR

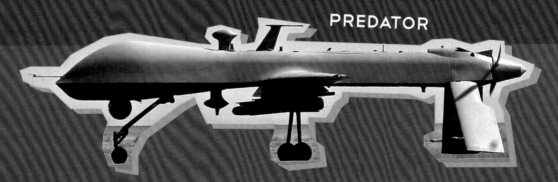

THE FATHER OF THE PREDATOR

Abraham Karem was born in Baghdad, Iraq, on June 27, 1937. Karem's family moved to Israel in 1951. He graduated with a degree in aircraft engineering and designed drones for the Israeli Air Force. In the late 1970s, Karem moved to the United States. He started a company called Leading Systems Inc., which would eventually be bought by General Atomics. General Atomics employed Karem to design a new UAV that would eventually become the Predator UAV. The Predator became one of the most effective and feared drones.

UAVs come in all shapes and sizes. Some, such as the RQ-11 Raven shown below, are small enough to be launched by hand like paper airplanes. Others, such as the Predator, are the size of small planes.

Spy drones are a valuable resource for the military. Drones can be launched over enemy territory, where they can remain for hours or even days, providing full-color, real-time video of enemy troops. These aircraft provide our troops with valuable information so they can plan their next move. Law enforcement agencies also use surveillance drones to search for and track criminals and **terrorists**.

SEARCH AND DESTROY

Drones greatly improve a military's ability to gather information about an enemy. They can sometimes provide an exact location where the enemy is hiding. However, even if the military can locate a target, it might not be possible for soldiers to get to it. That's why some drones are built for more active missions.

Drones used in combat situations are called unmanned combat aerial vehicles, or UCAVs. Combat drones may carry missiles and bombs, as well as the targeting computers needed to fire them. Because they need to carry heavy weapons, combat drones are usually fairly large—almost as large as regular aircraft. Two of the most common drones in the U.S. military's fleet are the MQ-1 Predator and the MQ-9 Reaper.

KNOW YOUR DRONES

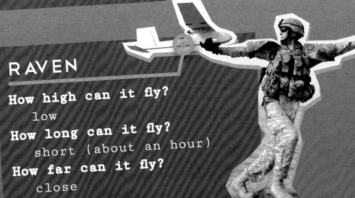

RAVEN

How high can it fly?
low

How long can it fly?
short (about an hour)

How far can it fly?
close

SHADOW

How high can it fly?
low to medium

How long can it fly?
medium (several hours)

How far can it fly?
line of sight

GLOBAL HAWK

How high can it fly?
medium to high

How long can it fly?
long (hours or days)

How far can it fly?
very far

The military uses different kinds of drones. Each drone has different strengths and is designed for different kinds of missions.

BOMB DISPOSAL AND HAZMAT

In addition to reconnaissance, military robots are used to locate, disarm, or dispose of explosives and other hazardous materials, or hazmats. Bomb disposal robots come in different shapes and sizes, but they have many features in common.

The PackBot and the TALON share a basic design. Both robots have an arm, cameras, and treaded wheels.

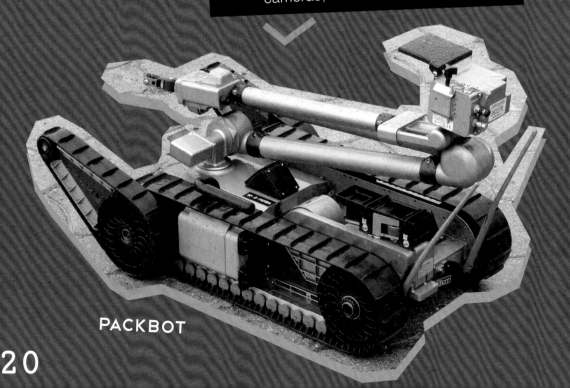

PACKBOT

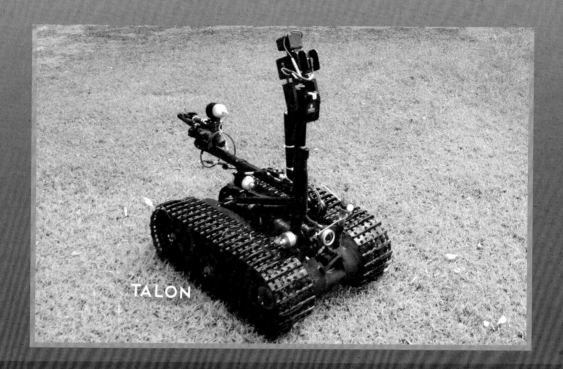

TALON

The MARCbot is one of the most common robots used to inspect suspicious objects. About the size of a big remote-controlled car, the MARCbot is small enough to look under furniture and vehicles. Similar robots include TALON robots, which come in different models and can be equipped for specific roles. Lights, cameras, and special sensors help the robots locate mines, improvised explosive devices (IEDs), and hazardous chemicals. Arms equipped with gripper claws allow these robots to move explosives and other dangerous objects away from soldiers and innocent civilians.

MOBILE WEAPON SYSTEMS

Drones aren't the only military robots used in combat situations. Years after military robots were used in World War I, modern armies use remote-operated weapon systems as well. The Gladiator tactical UGV is a mobile robotic system that may be used for surveillance, reconnaissance, and combat. Armed with machine guns and other automatic weapons, the Gladiator is intended to enter combat situations to minimize risks to human troops.

SWORDS were robots adapted from TALON robots. They could carry machine guns, automatic rifles, grenade launchers, or flamethrowers. They were one of the first types of robotic vehicles designed for combat. Companies have since designed similar robots, including MATILDA and MAARS, which could be used for combat. Human operators would control these machines remotely.

UGVs and remote-operated weapon systems such as SWORDS could save soldiers' lives on the front line.

23

URBAN WARFARE

Battlefields aren't always large, open spaces where two opposing armies clash during battle. In recent years, armed conflicts have shifted to cities and towns of varying sizes. Fighting a war in an urban landscape poses its own set of obstacles, including buildings, alleys, and the increased presence of innocent civilians.

Robots can be an important tool for soldiers fighting in urban environments. Drones can fly overhead and map out streets and buildings. Small ground robots, such as the PackBot and MARCbot, can be sent into areas ahead of soldiers to locate traps and enemy combatants. These robots can peek around corners, into windows, or even inside sewer pipes. Larger robots can break down doors, walls, and other obstacles, as well as carry additional equipment and supplies.

Some police departments use robots, such as the Andros, for SWAT (special weapons and tactics) operations. In addition to bomb disposal, police departments use these robots to break down doors and deliver food and supplies to **hostages**.

Drones are sometimes used to help locate people lost in the wilderness. This is often a job for law enforcement, but flying robots can be faster and more successful than human search parties. A single drone can search several miles in a matter of minutes, while it would take a human search party several hours. Unlike people, drones can search day and night. They can even see through clouds, rain, and fog.

Police departments around the world use drones that were once used by the military. Some police departments also use consumer quadcopters, such as the kinds you can buy online or at a local hobby shop.

Drones can also be used to help police search for suspected criminals. **Infrared** and low-light cameras can help police identify their targets at night or in bad weather. Drones can fly over a neighborhood and determine which buildings are occupied by sensing the heat given off by a human body. Drones are also cheaper than the helicopters and other aircraft often used by police departments.

Police departments, fire departments, and other emergency services are using robots to assist their efforts after accidents and natural disasters. After a natural disaster such as an earthquake or hurricane, survivors may be trapped. Small robots or flying drones can be sent into these areas to locate people who need help. Robots can be used to deliver water, medicine, and supplies to people waiting to be rescued.

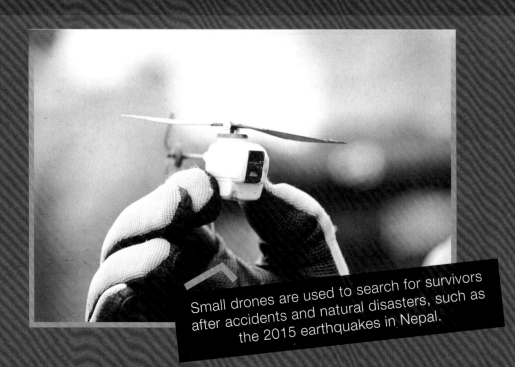

Small drones are used to search for survivors after accidents and natural disasters, such as the 2015 earthquakes in Nepal.

The U.S. Navy is testing a humanlike firefighting robot called SAFFiR. SAFFiR has special sensors that allow it to detect fires and see through smoke. When a fire is located, SAFFiR can use a fire hose to extinguish the flames. One day, firefighting robots like SAFFiR could be used to save the lives of civilian firefighters during wildfires.

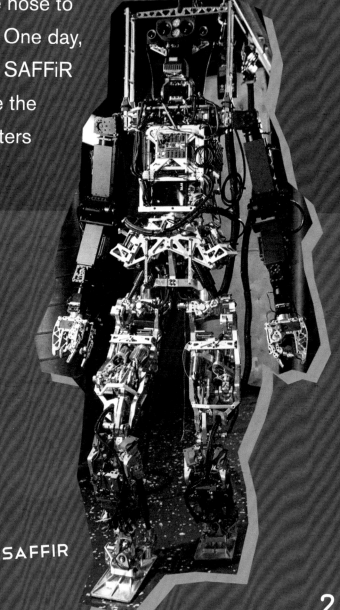

SAFFIR

THE FUTURE OF WARFARE

It's likely that the future will see more robots on the battlefield. Will we ever see a future when robot armies face each other in combat? Probably not. However, engineers are developing powered exosuits, which are wearable robots that could provide extra protection for human soldiers and allow them to carry more equipment and weapons.

Tomorrow's military robots won't be confined to land, either. The U.S. Navy is testing robots that can be used to locate underwater mines, inspect ships, and explore shipwrecks. DARPA is even developing a flying aircraft carrier from which fleets of unmanned aerial vehicles can be launched and recovered. Although robots have the power to be used against people in war, they also have the potential to save many lives.

GLOSSARY

civilian: A person not on active duty in the military.

combatant: A person, group, or country that fights in a war or battle.

console: A device by which an operator can control and monitor another device.

drone: A pilotless aircraft.

hostage: A person who is captured by someone who demands certain things before freeing the captured person.

infrared: Referring to rays of light that people can't see and are longer than rays that produce red light.

intelligence: The gathering of information about enemies.

joystick: A control device that allows motion in two or more directions.

mine: An explosive often buried in the ground or hidden underwater.

radiation: Waves of energy.

reconnaissance: The exploration of a place to collect information.

surveillance: The act of watching someone or something closely.

terrorist: One who uses violence and fear to achieve a political goal.

INDEX

WEBSITES

Due to the changing nature of Internet links, PowerKids Press has developed an online list of websites related to the subject of this book. This site is updated regularly. Please use this link to access the list: www.powerkidslinks.com/rar/mili